Living with a Visionary

i.m. Diana Adams Matthias

JOHN MATTHIAS

DOS MADRES

2021

DOS MADRES PRESS INC.
P.O. Box 294, Loveland, Ohio 45140
www.dosmadres.com   editor@dosmadres.com

Dos Madres is dedicated to the belief that the small press is essential to the vitality of contemporary literature as a carrier of the new voice, as well as the older, sometimes forgotten voices of the past. And in an ever more virtual world, to the creation of fine books pleasing to the eye and hand.

Dos Madres is named in honor of Vera Murphy and Libbie Hughes, the "Dos Madres" whose contributions have made this press possible.

Dos Madres Press, Inc. is an Ohio Not For Profit Corporation and a 501 (c) (3) qualified public charity. Contributions are tax deductible.

Executive Editor: Robert J. Murphy

Illustration & Book Design: Elizabeth H. Murphy
www.illusionstudios.net
Cover: Collage of *Snow Storm: Steam-Boat off a Harbour's Mouth*,
Joseph Mallord William Turner, (1842)
and *Diana*, marble bust by Hiram Powers, 1853

Typeset in Adobe Garamond Pro, Goudy Old Style & Aquiline
ISBN 978-1-953252-38-8
Library of Congress Control Number: 2021945541

CONTENTS

Author's Note — v

I : *Three Poems*

Rhododendron — 3
Of Artemis, Aging — 5
Good Dream — 6

II : *Living with a Visionary*

You would think it was a performance — 13

III : *Some of Her Things*

I was standing in the middle of a river — 29

Afterword by Igor Webb — 39

About the Authors — 47

Author's Note

This little book is published as a memorial to my late wife, Diana. I have written many poems to or about her during fifty years of marriage, as well as a certain amount of prose. The title section was published in the *New Yorker* on February 1, 2021. The essay must have touched a nerve among many readers, as I received literally hundreds of responses to the piece—email, old-fashioned mail in envelopes, phone calls, poems, even prayers—and I am not even yet finished answering all of them. I found the experience of hearing from so many readers very strange and utterly overwhelming. Many of those who wrote wanted to tell me their own stories, some of which were very painful to read. What I promised these readers was that I would try within a year to publish the essay in a context more permanent than the back issue of a magazine, even one as esteemable as the *New Yorker*. This booklet is an attempt to do that.

Besides "Living with a Visionary," I include three poems at the beginning, and a kind of prose poem at the end. "Rhododendron" was written when Diana was still in her thirties. She was in her mid-sixties when I wrote "Of Artemis, Aging," which was dedicated to her in *Complayntes for Doctor Neuro and Other Poems*. "Good Dream" is the last section of the title piece of that collection, but appears here as a freestanding poem. As the title of the sequence suggests, we were by this time struggling together with, and sometimes against, Diana's neurologists after she had begun her battle with Parkinson's in her early seventies. The "Good Dream" of that poem prefigures the nightmare we inhabited that is described in the essay.

"Some of Her Things" might be considered a kind of coda to "Living with a Visionary." It is much more consciously an artefact than is the essay, which was in fact first written simply to tell family members and friends what had happened to us. It is a strange thing that something intended to have very few readers ended up having so many.

I : *Three Poems*

Rhododendron

Several years ago, you planted
Near my study window something green.
Today I notice it, not just green,

But blazing red-in-green exactly
Like the rhododendron it turned out
To be when you said: *Look!*

My rhododendron's flowering.
As usual, I had never asked, had
Never noticed, would not have

Had an answer if our daughter or
Her friend had said a day ago: *and that?*
Just what is that? It's something green,

I'd have had to say, *that your mother*
Planted there, some kind of flower
That hasn't flowered yet, although

She planted it three years ago.
It's the word itself, I think, that's
Made it flower, and your saying it.

The winter's not been easy, and the
Spring's been slow. I stared at long white
Papers full of emptiness and loss

As one might stare at rows of narrow
Gardens full of snow. The words
Have not come easily, have not come well.

Easily, you tell me, stepping through
The door: *Look! My rhododendron's
Flowering* . . . And it is, and it does.

Of Artemis, Aging . . .

(For Diana, on her 65th birthday)

But of course she does not age! Immortal, she
Does what she has always done: There is no future tense
To drag her down, to soften her hard body,
Compromise her chastity. Through the ages she is
What she always is: There is no past except for those
She touches, touched, will touch: They rise and fall
With time, but she is timeless. Does she envy them
Their human grace to change? Callisto, found with child,
Became a constellation with her son, Arktos, rising up
Behind her in the circumpolar sky. Actaeon turned
Into a stag. I've seen Diana at her bath but never was
Devoured by my hounds, only by my longing.
Young, she moved like the wife of Menelaos in the
Eyes of Telemakhos—*straight as a shaft of gold.*
But even Helen by that time had changed: Housefrau
In the great Lakedaimon mansion house, she began
To age. The red-haired king found his lady all the more
Amazing and the struggle on the beachhead year by year
Receded in his memory. Vindictive Artemis forgets
Nothing and does not forgive. Her eternal present
Is as sterile as the moon's. If she could change, she
Might be like the woman called by her Roman name
Reading in a book beside the fire in my own house.
She has come down all these years with me, and she
Is getting old. She turns the pages slowly, then looks up.
Her wise ironic glance is *straight as a shaft of gold.*

Good Dream

Good dream, good dream. Thank you
Spirits of the night. Her tormentors often
Do not spare her sleep, but last night's
Visitors did not disturb her, wreck
Her back or wrack her with the thrashing,
Make her shout out anything obscene
At all, and so I too could sleep, wrapped
Around her like an adolescent lover.

It's not that I'd been reading Ovid
Who can be as cruel in his metamorphoses
As some malign neurologist, turning
Living things into grotesques. But I feel
Certain I was visited. You'll laugh when
I tell you Zeus and Hermes were
The strangers at my door, but it is true.
Oh, of course they did not look like gods.

They looked like homeless folk, they
Looked like vagrants, like people one sees
Sleeping on the street in cardboard weather-breaks,
In old sweaters, greatcoats from the First
World War. (You'll find them there in Ovid VIII,
But I only understood that when I woke.
A gentle, generous story; rare enough and lovely
In his book. Baucis and Philemon.)

Who were my visitors? *We're fugitives,*
They sang together. But what lovely harmony!
Sounds more strange than Wolpe's, something
From another world. It was as if Abraham
And Isaac sang together walking toward an altar.
We're survivors of the war, the pogrom,
Revolution, plague, they sang. *Will you give us food?*
I said I would if only they kept singing.

I knew they were two gods in spite of what
They sang to me. *We're criminals,* they sang.
And now you must protect us, lie for us,
Offer us asylum, compromise your lives. We're ill.
How far will you go to enter our disease?
You value ease. We're here to violate all that.
We're vile, but you cannot sing yourself to being
Otherwise than by embracing us.

I pulled up wicker chairs, invited them
To sit, speared a fish with a two-tined pole from
A river that came flowing through one door
And out the other; one wall fell away revealing
Children playing by a lake our river seemed
To feed, and, three-walled only, yet the house stood
Firm and somehow firmer than it ever had before.
I found an oak leaf growing from my hand.

Goblets full of wine appeared; the oak leaf, falling,
Spread itself as tablecloth, expanding. And they sang:
Misfortune is your fortune, disorder all your order
Here. We like a house with books all over,
Manuscripts and papers in a clutter, pens leaking
Ink in pockets of discarded shirts, paintings
Hanging crooked on the wall, the wall's plaster
Cracked and open outwards for the nests of birds.

But we have never had a home ourselves
And so we ask for berries that Athena cherishes,
Endive and radishes, curdled cheese, that fish;
We ask for grapes and apples afterwards,
A comb of honey; most of all good conversation
While we eat and drink. I somehow put these
Things before them, found the fish had cooked
Although I never put it on the fire.

I asked them, were they hunted? They sang *O yes,*
By you, and also others: Jacks and Jills,
Baucis and Philemon. By the mad who lie
On gurneys in the dark halls of institutions,
Roll in wheel chairs to groves in city parks, suck
Nutrition from the bottles full of drips that flow
Into their veins through tubes like straws they
Once shared in soda glasses with their pretty girls.

Did you know that Aesculapius arrives
In dreams as an enormous snake journeying from
Epidaurus twisted round the high mast of a ship
Summoned by us to this river by the lake? But look.
The three remaining walls of my house collapsed
And I was standing in a marble temple, and I
Was not I. Beside me, Serpent Aesculapius arose
In flaming cloak. Diana spoke: *I am a linden tree*
And what I was replied: *I have become an oak.*

II : *Living with a Visionary*

You would think it was a performance of some kind. When she wakes up, if she has slept at all, she tells me about the giants carrying trees and bushes on what she calls zip lines, which I am able to identify as telephone wires. Beneath the busy giants, she explains, there is a marching band playing familiar tunes by John Philip Sousa. She is not especially impressed by either of these things, and the various children playing games in the bedroom annoy her. "Out you go," she says to them. Then she describes the man with no legs who spent the night lying beside her in bed. He had been mumbling in pain, but nobody would come to help him. She remembers her own pain, too. "I could hardly move," she says.

And she can hardly move now. Her legs are stiff, her back is cracking as I lift her out of bed. Although still clearly in pain, she gives me a sly look and gestures with her chin toward the flowerpot in the hallway. "The Flowery Man," she says. "He's very nice."

She is fully articulate, in many ways her familiar self. She asks me if I saw the opera. I'm not sure which opera she means; we've seen many over the fifty years that we've been married. She means the one last night in our back yard. She describes it in detail—the stage set, the costumes, the "really amazing" lighting, the beautiful voices. I ask her what opera was performed. Now I get another look, not a sly one but a suspicious one.

"You don't believe me, do you?"

I say that it's not a matter of belief but of perception. I can't see what she sees. She tells me that this is a great pity. I miss so much of life. I used to have something of an imagination, but I've evidently lost it. Maybe she should start

13

spending time with someone else. Also, she knows about my girlfriend. The one in the red jacket. There is no girlfriend, but there is a red jacket hanging over the back of her walker. Suddenly, she forgets the girlfriend and remembers the opera. "Oh," she says. "It was 'La Traviata,' and we went together with Anna Natrebko before she sang."

Now I have my own brief vision. Diana is only twenty-one, I am twenty-five. We have just arrived in South Bend, where I am teaching English at Notre Dame. A friend wrote about us in those days as having appeared to him like two fawns in the grove of our local Arcadia. Diana wore the clothes she had brought from England, including her miniskirt, and people in cars would honk their horns and stare. In London, where we had met, it had been the middle of the nineteen-sixties; at our Midwestern college, it was more like the fifties. A former student told me that when I held classes at home, for a change of scene, he and his classmates took bets on who would be lucky enough to talk to her.

I see her walking in from the kitchen with tea and her homemade scones. College boys—only boys were admitted back then—lift china cups balanced on wafer-thin saucers. Some have never eaten a crumbly scone or sipped tea out of such a delicate cup. Diana is often told she looks like Julie Christie, and my students all want to be Omar Shariff, Christie's co-star in "Doctor Zhivago." Some write poems inspired by Lara, Zhivago's muse. Diana smiles at them, greeting those whose names she remembers. Hello, Vince. Hi there, Richard. She dazzles them. She dazzles me.

Art was her passion. Later, she earned an art history degree and became the curator of education at our university's museum. She devised a program of what she called "curriculum-structured tours," ambitiously proposing to organize museum tours that would be relevant to any class. This she did—chemistry students learned about the properties of seventeenth-century paint, psychology majors studied portraits for signs of their subjects' mental health— and eventually she exported her innovations to other college campuses. Because of her, students began looking seriously at paintings and sculptures. They followed her hand, pointing out some luminous detail; they listened to the music of her voice, her British accent slowly becoming Americanized over the decades.

Diana trained a new set of gallery interns each year, teaching them about all there was to see and find in the museum's art. She loved them dearly, and they loved her back. She had been conducting tours for thirty years when a former intern, Maria, came by the house—ostensibly on an errand to collect some of Diana's library books. Really, she wanted to talk to me. She explained that Diana had started seeing things. The first time Maria noticed it, Diana was showing a class of French students a reduction of Charles Louis-Lucien Müller's "The Roll Call of the Last Victims of the Reign of Terror," from 1860. It's a very busy painting, with dozens of figures waiting to be transported to the guillotine. Diana told the students that at the center of "The Roll Call" was a man named General Marius. But General Marius wasn't there; he was around the corner, in a painting called "Marius and the Gaul," about which Diana had written her thesis, many years before. She was speaking in French, and at first Maria thought that Diana had got tangled up in the language. Surely it was her words, not her reality, that had become so confused.

Not too long after Maria's visit, Diana returned home one day looking tired and depressed. She sat down on the sofa next to me, took my hand, and said, "The students tell me that I'm seeing things that aren't there." I admitted that Maria had already told me about this. By then, Diana had begun treatment for Parkinson's disease, taking a standard cocktail of medicines in small amounts: levodopa combined with carbidopa, in a drug called Sinemet. She had received the diagnosis only because her doctor couldn't otherwise explain her onset of general weakness. Aside from fatigue, she had virtually no symptoms, and her behavior had been absolutely normal while taking Sinemet. Now she confessed that she was seeing things at home as well. She pointed at a wadded-up sweater on a chair across the room. "That's not really a cat, is it?"

I asked her what else she saw. "Little people," she explained, "like Gulliver's Lilliputians." Objects had been changing shape—"morphing" was her word—for some time, but recently things had begun appearing out of nowhere. We saw a specialist in Chicago, who, like the neurologists Eric Ahlskog and Oliver Sacks, called these "illusions." We suspected that the hallucinations were a side effect of Sinemet, and, after consulting many books and articles, Diana and I began to titrate her medication ourselves. Most Parkinson's patients end up doing this, experimenting with how much they take of each medicine and at what time. There were several new delivery systems for the basic mix of levodopa and carbidopa, and we tried them all, along with a number of adjuvant therapies.

At first, Diana could identify her illusions as such,

and sometimes even dismiss them. ("Scat!" got rid of the cat.) The things she saw were not always frightening. Many of them seemed inspired by her work in the visual arts. Visiting a neighbor, Diana enthusiastically described a painting on a blank wall where, we later learned, one had been hanging until several days before. Her knowledge of eighteenth-century art may in part explain her delight in seeing topiary figures cut into very large trees, where I saw nothing but leaves. Some of the visions she told me about were clearly breathtaking. "If only you could see this," she said.

I couldn't see what she saw, but I could see her. She was somehow growing more beautiful—or beautiful in a new way. Everyone noticed this. Never one to use much makeup or even visit a hair stylist, she would wash her face in the morning, put up her hair or let it hang at shoulder length, and come downstairs to start her day. Her striking good looks belied the condition that would bring her down. It was Julie Christie all over again, but not from "Doctor Zhivago"; she was the aging Christie of Sally Polly's movie "Away from Her." Adapted from Alice Munro's story "The Bear Came Over the Mountain," the film is about a woman with Alzheimer's disease. Her decline is slow, until it is suddenly fast. Diana watched the movie without anxiety. She had not, so far, suffered any significant memory loss. When I reminded her that decades earlier my students had compared her to the actress, she laughed. During a trip to Chicago to see her doctor, we had been approached by a man on the street, who said, "I just have to tell you how beautiful you are. Forgive me for intruding on your day." We got into a taxi, and Diana growled to me, "I sure don't feel very beautiful."

For two or three years, Diana's condition was manageable through modifications in her medications, and through her ability to recognize the hallucinations for what they were. At the art gallery, she avoided confusion by writing out scripts for her tours. She managed to retire when she was scheduled to, not before. It was shortly afterward that her hallucinations began to increase in frequency and intensity. She insisted that the topiary trees were the work of giants, and she described the giants' elaborate uniforms. Plays and operas were staged in our back yard, spontaneous parades appeared in the streets.

It became harder and harder for her to understand that her visions were not real. She sometimes asked me why these events were not written about in the paper or covered in the news on television. In the house, nothing held still: objects danced on the mantel, the ideograms on our hanging scroll of Chinese calligraphy flew around like butterflies. At the beginning, many of these transformations had given her pleasure. More and more, however, they annoyed and alarmed her. Three women were "hanging" in her closet and refused to leave. The Flowery Man roamed the house. There were rude people who masturbated into a dresser drawer and had sex on the living room sofa.

When Diana could no longer shake these things off, she began to surrender to them. She slowly ceased to see them as hallucinations. I had read that it did not help to deny the reality of these visions, so I stopped doing that. I began trying to deal with them as if I could see what she did. Friends were encouraged to make the same allowances. For a while this helped. A fifth person at a dinner for four did not pose a big problem once you got used to this kind of thing. I informed members of Diana's reading group that she might refer to people who weren't there, and they, too, made the adjustment.

One day, she shouted for my help. A housepainter in his white overalls, she told me, was painting over the portrait of one of our daughters that hung on the living room wall. The man didn't speak; none of Diana's human apparitions ever spoke, though their mouths would move without sound, and sometimes they would respond to stern rebukes. I could say things like "I'll see the painter to the door." But often the damage had been done. In the case of our daughter's portrait, it continued to exist, for Diana, partially erased. She referred to the painting as "the half-faced child."

Some medications work for Parkinson's patients with hallucinations, but for Diana they all seemed to make things worse. In November of 2019, a new kind of confusion about both space and time took hold. One morning, I found her with her suitcase packed, ready to travel. When I asked where she was going, she wasn't sure. "Away," she said. She wasn't sure why. But, she insisted, "we certainly can't stay any longer in this person's house, in a place where we don't even speak the language."

Christmas approaches, and I return to the present tense. Everything that happens after this feels like it's still happening now. Slowly, through the winter, Diana's benign hallucinations become terrible and threatening presences. (Meanwhile, in China, a new and deadly virus is unleashed on the world.) Diana loses her ability to sleep, a common

19

and debilitating feature of Parkinson's. Because she is either sleepless or tormented by nightmares, I am also unable to sleep. For a while, I am able to soothe her and offer comfort, but often her dreams continue unabated when she wakes up. Eventually, I am simply incorporated into them. When I ask her if she is awake, she says she does not know.

Her eating also becomes a problem, and I know that she is not getting proper nutrition. I use the blender again and again, counting calories, mixing in anything containing protein. She is getting very thin. I sleep only when she sleeps and eat a quick sandwich as I cook for her. She looks at me one morning and says, "Who are you? What are you doing here?"

Because Diana hides things, then promptly forgets where they are, I find myself searching for her medical insurance cards, her driver's license, some kind of I.D. with her picture on it. She sends me on a wild-goose chase all over the house. This drawer. That closet. But I can never find what we need. The hallucinated people begin to take on more life than the living. And they have names. Not generic and rather charming names like the Flowery Man but monosyllabic American names like Bob, Pete, Dick, George, Jack. No one seems to have a surname. "Jack who?" I ask her. She gives me a straight look and says, "Jack the Ripper." She keeps asking, "Who's in charge?" I wish I knew.

In March, as the pandemic descends on the Midwest, I try to explain why she cannot go out or see friends. She doesn't understand. I don't dare leave her alone, even for a short trip to the grocery store. She begins going outside when my back is turned, and she frightens some of the neighbors with things she claims to see. I make rules. No phoning friends after 10 P.M. No going outdoors after bed or going downstairs for breakfast in the middle of the night. I finally move to a bed in a separate room.

With the country in lockdown, I can no longer reach Diana's neurologist in Chicago. Local doctors help us refill some of her medications over the telephone, but have nothing to offer that might help the dementia that is now clearly part of the picture. My most recent reading makes me wonder whether she might not have Parkinson's but something called Lewy body dementia, which produces vivid hallucinations. Its terrifying symptoms are believed to have led to the suicide of the actor Robin Williams. Diana talks about "jumping in the river." (The St. Joseph River is only a few hundred yards from our front door.) Neighbors offer to do some shopping for us, but as the pandemic gets worse, I hesitate to ask them for more help. When I finally make contact with two or three "senior helper" organizations, I am told that all their programs are on hold. I can do nothing but try to continue on my own. I begin taking pills myself— sedatives washed down with glasses of Merlot. We are living on cans of beans and prescription drugs.

There are still moments when Diana is very happy. Sometimes, she seems to be in a state of bliss. She stands at the open doorway and gazes into the sky. I stand behind her. "Look!" she says. "Why can't you see?" I tell her that I'm trying, but maybe need some help. She becomes angry and shouts, "The gods! The gods!"

One day, I find Diana clutching a balled-up blanket to her breast. "What have you got?" I ask her. "A dead baby," she says. I have never seen such terror in her eyes. I have never seen it in anybody's eyes.

At some point—a day later, two days later—police arrive at the door. In the street, an ambulance is flashing its colored lights. The three policemen at the door have masks on, and I'm initially frightened by this, because I don't know that many people are now wearing them. Someone has called the police about a lady who lives here who may need to go to the hospital. I stand there gazing stupidly at the policemen. They ask if they can talk to the lady. I tell them she's my wife. Diana is on the sofa, more or less catatonic.

When I step onto the front porch, I notice some of our neighbors watching from their yards. I am asked questions about Diana and who has been looking after her. I begin to fear that I'm about to be arrested. Someone suggests that maybe it would be good for her to be completely checked out in the E.R., and possibly admitted for a day or so. The next thing I know, two of the ambulance men are bringing a stretcher up to the porch. One of them asks if he can talk to my wife. Finally, I'm able to say something. I say no. They are immediately suspicious. To my amazement, I hear Diana saying, "I'll talk to them. It's O.K." They ask her what's wrong. She describes a few of her hallucinations. She's worried about what's happened to the dead baby. What dead baby? I try to intervene, but already she's explaining that she had the dead baby in her arms just a moment ago. Perhaps it has rolled away. She gets down on one knee and reaches under the sofa. "Oh, good," she says, reappearing with the blanket. "Here it is."

While the medics are conferring with one another, Diana suddenly says, "I think I should go to the hospital." The ambulance guys seem delighted by this. Diana is put on the stretcher, and the ambulance disappears. No one asks what I think should be done. No one asks me to come along. In the confusion, the blanket has been left on the front porch. When everyone is gone, I take it inside.

That night, Diana is admitted to the hospital for observation. I won't be able to visit her, however, because of COVID restrictions. I am frantic: they'll get all the Parkinson's meds mixed up, they don't know her schedule. What will happen if she misses a dose of Sinemet?

What transpires in the next days and weeks is sometimes vividly clear and sometimes swirling in a surrealistic fog. At some point, it is decided that I, too, should be examined in the hospital. In the E.R., I am told that I am suffering from exhaustion, malnutrition, and dehydration. I end up on the same floor as Diana. By the time I arrive, she has told everyone that she is a movie director working on a documentary about art therapy in hospitals. From my bed, I explain to her doctors, who are different from my own, as much of her medical history as I can. I am allowed to talk to Diana only by phone.

Social workers keep appearing with documents for me to sign. My daughter Laura and I have agreed, in theory, that eventually Diana will have to move into an assisted-living community. A new facility for patients with dementia has recently been built near Laura's house, in Worthington, Ohio. Laura wants to take Diana there, and I have to admit that I am no longer able to look after her. I am barely able to look after myself. I sign the papers giving Laura power of attorney for Diana and me. There are decisions to be made, bills to be paid, and I am flat on my back in the hospital.

COVID is tearing through the country. The hospital is filling up with patients, my bed is in demand. My doctors ask if I want to be sent home or to spend three days in the psychiatric hospital associated with the general hospital where I am being treated. They talk about rest, recovery.

Where I end up is not a health spa but more like a boot camp. Before I am moved, all of my possessions are taken away. No shoelaces, no belt. At the new facility, I am given a handful of large and small pills every three hours. At night, all patients are on suicide watch. I barely sleep. While I am in the psych ward, Diana is driven in a long-distance ambulance to the care facility in Ohio, where, after a fourteen-day quarantine, she will now live. How Diana deals with this news, what she understands and doesn't understand, I do not know. She still thinks she is directing a documentary film. I am not allowed to see her before she leaves.

In the second psych ward where I find myself remanded, I am the oldest patient by far. The program of endless group therapies seems designed for adolescents. At seventy-nine, I am too weak to do many of the things demanded of me. When I do not immediately respond to the pills I'm given, there is talk of electroconvulsive therapy. I object, and an online hearing is convened, where a judge concludes that, although I must stay beyond the hospital's mandatory seventy-two-hour observation period, I do not have to undergo shock therapy.

Meanwhile, I am terrified of COVID. Locked out of our rooms for most of the day, we are all in one another's way, and patients share a common bathroom. One day, I am required to cut off my beard. Looking at myself in the mirror, I discover the corners of my mouth locked in a permanent grimace. The beard has hidden this from me: I can't smile.

I try to explain to the staff that there has been some

kind of mistake, that I need to rescue my wife, who has been taken to Ohio. The things I say to the nurses and therapists must sound mad. When I am finally allowed to see the chief psychiatrist, I hear the desperation in my voice. I watch the unbelieving faces of everyone around me, and wonder how often Diana saw the same incredulity in my own face.

Somehow, our family lawyer gets in touch with a woman named Mary, a registered nurse and "personal health-care advocate," who is the one to finally secure my release from the psychiatric facility. I am asked to sign some papers that I haven't read, and then I am free. On the way home in an ambulance, driving back the same way Diana came, I consider asking the attendants riding alongside me if they have heard of the Flowery Man, the topiary trees, the little people—any of Diana's hallucinated cast of characters. For years I have tried as hard as I could to see these things, to share Diana's view of the passing world. In her absence, returning to the home where I must now begin to live by myself, I long all the more to understand the reality that she inhabits.

When COVID insinuated itself into the facility in Worthington, Ohio, in November, I had been at home for five months. For a couple of weeks, I had managed to communicate with Diana through screens. This confused her, though, so we started using the telephone instead. The last time I saw her face was on Zoom. She told me that she had something beginning with the letter "C." Then she suddenly smiled her wonderful smile. "What a sweet little girl," she said, following a hallucination with a sharp turn of her head.

Diana almost survived COVID. After testing positive, she spent several nights at the hospital, but was sent back to her facility with a normal temperature and a negative test result. For a few days, I was able to imagine seeing her again, even touching her. I had it all figured out. I would be among the first in line to be vaccinated, among the first to embrace a loved one who had been unreachable for so long. I didn't care how many hallucinated people came along, as long as Diana was around to see them.

Then her blood-oxygen level dropped. She was not likely to live through the night. Laura put the phone to Diana's ear, and I read the first poem I ever wrote for her—about waking together in a small Left Bank hotel in Paris before we were married. Finally, I started reading from a book of poetry I had written about her struggle. The dedicatory poem is about the Greek goddess Artemis, known by the Romans as Diana. Its final lines return to Diana the mortal, my wife:

> If she could change, she
> Might be like the woman called by her Roman name
> Reading in a book beside the fire in my own house.
> She has come down all these years with me.

I couldn't continue. "You're doing great, Dad," my daughter said, "but she wants to know about the Flowery Man." So I told her everything I knew.

III : *Some of Her Things*

I was standing in the middle of a river. In waist high water and afraid that I would lose my footing and be swept downstream where the river is deep enough to drown in. What I had to do was difficult. My job was to sort things in a giant case as big as all the world that nonetheless was floating there beside me. In it were Diana's things—her dresses, her family heirlooms, her intimate apparel; also all her past; her houses and her hats; her dislikes and her likes; her looks and what she'd overlooked; her locks and keys. Although I knew she had died, she was fully present on the north bank of the St. Joseph River with its bend to the south that gave the town its name. South Bend was not her native town, nor the St. Joseph River her own. Her own rivers were in Suffolk, in England—the Alde, the Orwell, and the Deben. Still, there she was; and everything besides was in the case. *Do like Henry James,* she shouted. But I didn't know what Henry James had done. Outside only she and I, the river and the riverbank. *Do like Henry James,* she shouted once again. *But save me seven things.*

1.

I find that Henry James saved nothing. None of Constance Woolson's things. Her middle name, Fenimore, tended to be recognized. She was an independent woman but maybe in love with James. Maybe James knew or maybe not. If it was the case, that is, and the world is everything that is the case. They would meet in Venice, Florence, London. They both loved Venice best. Her books sold better than his. She was going deaf. When she went to the opera she heard no singing. But still she went, alone. And was seen. She moved from Casa Biondetti to Casa Semitecolo in Venice. When she threw herself out the window of the latter—was it for unrequited love? Her gondolier was called Tito. Tito the gondolier. She had collected many things during her life. Which had no life of their own and someone had to make a case, execute a plan. Like you, she liked magnolia trees in bloom. Tito knew the lagoon where only the best gondoliers could navigate in safety. Henry James and Tito took her clothing out in the boat. They had decided to drown her dresses and gowns. Henry tossed Miss Woolson's things in the lagoon and Tito pushed them under with his long heavy pole. A ball gown billowed up and wouldn't sink. It seemed that Constance Fenimore Woolson swam beside them now. *The first thing I'll save is your magnolia tree.*

2.

When our daughter was young a teacher asked in class, what's a punt? Laura said it's like a boat. The other children laughed, mentally punting their footballs. It's when you can't make first down and have to give the other side the ball. Laura said, it's like a gondola. I was awkward with the pole and indecisive, unlike Tito on the Grand Canal or the lagoon. We were on the Cam in our punt and had to turn around once we had reached Grantchester. Poll it left or right? Poll's a verb, and also a noun. Punt's a long and narrow craft. Craft has several meanings, several anythings are maybe just in case. In case you wondered, in case you pay attention. Dr. Leavis tried beside the Cam explaining literary criticism to Wittgenstein. The latter said he didn't see the point. Of literary criticism. Dr. Leavis didn't think a punt involved a football. There were certain lawns at Cambridge colleges where Dr. Leavis couldn't take a step. I myself nearly knocked him into the street coming out of The Whim in 1966. The Whim was a tea shop. In 1966 I also met Diana. We were that very afternoon to punt our way to Grantchester. Just the two of us. Not with Wittgenstein or Leavis either one. *I'll save your black Schrödinger cat called Zeitgeist.*

3.

We sailed on the Alde. No punt this time, a real sailor's sailing boat. I mean it belonged to the Captain. When you sail the Alde from Orford you get the wind from the sea, the river running near it, tidal and tricky for the helmsman. If the tide goes out on you, you'll spend the night on a mudbank. You won't jump out because you'd sink in it like quicksand. The sale of some things in England made us sad; but I am even sadder standing in the St. Joseph River. This time all things must go downstream aside from the excepted seven. Otherwise that is the case. I reach into the case for Henry James's *American* and send him doing backstroke down the stream. Life is but a dram of chance. A drachm should you have a drachma. Trying to come about we broke a stay. The sail shivered and it caught no wind. Winded when I ran to meet her, late but with my arms full of roses, Captain Adams said, it's jolly well my boat but she can sail it with you in or out. I was out and in. We would go alas to a landlocked docking port our destination on a Greyhound bus. Best not complain. *I'll save for you your father's sailing boat.*

4.

Docked and disembarking we found ourselves a real presence at a Catholic university. There was a good story thereabouts. In years gone by the KKK was anti-Catholic not just anti-black. Once their busses parked in this same lot and members marched to what they thought would be a rally. All the ND football toughs had gathered round the corner from their destination and, as they arrived, torches alight and chanting Nazi slogans, the students set upon them with their fists, fending off their clubs with field hockey sticks. The KKK retreated, beaten black and blue. In that first year we found the work of Ivan Meštrović at every turn. He'd come here like an exile fleeing Kosovo. He did not play football. His Pièta was in the church, Christ at Jacob's Well outside the window where I taught my first group of students, all of whom became my friends. People gathered at the well in springtime and among them stood my pagan wife, a friend of all my friends. They laughed and drank together from the well. Elsewhere on these grounds Meštrović had carved Persephone and Dionysius in a single block of stone. In Eleusinian rites Persephone's betrothed to brother-son. I'd be her brother-son and spouse. I was. A girl of springtime steps out of the Pentateuch's five scrolls. *I'll save you all the wine in Jacob's well.*

5.

I can't save everything. I couldn't even save you from your illness. Is illness in the case that floats beside me? I see silk and cotton garments, I see wool. I see scarves that might be veils. I see vials of unguents and of poisons too. There's lace here also and some boxes within boxes as if Russian dolls. A small travelling case, a gold half-hunter pocket watch. Loose pages, sketches with a stick of charcoal, sharpened pencils, watercolor paints. Grandmother was the artist. Could have been professional but was an Edwardian lady, European traveler, scribbler in her diary. But she did have shows. She wouldn't sell, but gave away her work if someone really liked it. She was ninety when your mother Pamela was nine. They watched from Fife surrender of the German fleet, scuttled one year later full fathom five. 1914–1918 war. In the boxes within boxes medals for the men, and for the women ribbons from a horse and pony show. Someone's lock of hair tied up with a ribbon. Your half-sister's wedding dress. Daguerreotypes of Hilton-Youngs and Drury-Lowes and Bonham-Carters. Double-barreled through the generations until now. The first Lord Kennet tried to court Virginia Woolf (Virginia Stephen then). The last box of all contains some teeth. Louisa saved her teeth, and I guess was toothless when at ninty she beheld surrender of the German fleet. *I'll save you now your granddad's grandest prize—it's a By God Authentic Victoria Cross.*

6.

Twelve VCs by Breakfast is the title of the book about Zeebrugge. The Zeebrugge raid. My own VC that stood for Very Cautious led you to impatience and you whispered in my ear. I said I feared impetuosity. You kissed me on the cheek. I was lucky to have known about the U-boats operating out of Bruges. I'd found them in the mouth of a canal where from the Belgian harbor they would sail into the sea. The North Sea, under which was Doggerland which once between two icesheets had allowed for walking with your deer's antler harpoon in search of anything that was the case in the Holocene. But it was a mole in April of 1918. A mole with German guns protecting the narrow mouth of the canal. Along with the VCs your father's men won DSOs and DSCs. There were framed pictures of his ship above the fireplace, where soon we settled down to kiss in earnest. That was April 1966. Computer generated maps have shown where Doggerland emerged and flourished following the last Age of Ice. The ice was broken, as they say. *I'll save the secret that you whispered in my ear.*

7.

The river that I'm standing in was also glacier-carved. The Erie ice, the Saginaw, the Michigan converged just here. Hills and ranges fixed the contours then. Basins formed, and runoff made two rivers wider than the Mississippi. Tributaries broke through lateral moraines. The Elkhart and the Yellow Rivers drained away the last of Maumee glacier—no waters yet could run off to Desplaines. When they did, the two great rivers slowed, silted up their valleys with debris and changed their names. Turning on itself, Dowagiac became its former tributary, flowing to Lake Michigan. Kankakee at flood time emptied into the immense abandoned channel, flowed on to St. Joseph, left an ice gorge, then a sand bar and a bluff. I suppose I stand midstream only in a dream, but I am broken to the point that I can't tell. I hear a bell I know rings from St. Mary's. I've sent downstream all everything except the seven things I now will list. The case is closed. *I'll save this bit of ice right in my heart.*

The first thing I'll save is your magnolia tree

The next thing I'll save is your Schrödinger cat called Zeitgeist

I'll save for you your father's sailing boat

I'll save you all the wine in Jacob's well

I'll save your granddad's grandest prize: A By God Authentic Victoria Cross

I'll save your secret whispered in my ear

I'll save this bit of ice right in my heart

AFTERWORD

AFTERWORD
Igor Webb

Collected here are a remarkable—lovely but also wrenching—group of love poems from a man to his wife.[1] The poet, editor, and translator John Matthias met Diana Adams while on a Fulbright to London in the fall of 1966, and not many months later the couple married in an old church near Diana's family home in Hacheston, Suffolk. At the time of Diana's death in late November 2020, they had been married for over fifty years. I have called these works love poems, which they are. But the love story is shadowed by affliction. Around eight years before her death Diana began to show the symptoms of what was eventually diagnosed as Parkinson's, the harrowing disease which, along with Covid-19, finally took her life. These are love poems in the haunting form of laments. The lament, uttered when love and death are most closely bound, is something like an essential accessory to mortality. It is at the same time the most unsettling, even the most embarrassing form, exposing what we aren't supposed to see. The Athenian audience at the Dionysia festival of 415 BCE didn't award Euripides's searing *The Trojan Women*, the outstanding lament of Greek drama, first prize, and who can be surprised—the play offers no salve for its endless series of deaths, no tragic resignation, no redemption, no dignified exit. Only lamentation, the

---

1   A longer version of this afterword, under the title "Matthias' Laments," appeared in *The Fortnightly Review*, n.s., 35.

wailing arias of Hecuba, Cassandra, Andromache . . . But it is not the first prize play of that Dionysia, by Xenocles, that we are still reading today, because *The Trojan Women* demonstrates beautifully, if that's the word, the particular authority of the lament, which is that it offers solace by rendering grief as art.

Joseph Brodsky, writing about what once were the most famous laments in English—Thomas Hardy's "Poems 1912–13," on the sudden death of his wife of thirty-eight years, Emma Gifford—observes that "craftsmanship was a no lesser issue for the poet here than the issue itself."[2] Craftsmanship was an issue for Hardy, as it is for Matthias, because the lament will not do its work for either writer or reader if it is not wholly natural—an unalloyed confession—and wholly artificial, that is, formally masterful. But the catch, for the writer, is that there is no time left to hazard practice in the discipline: you just have to do it, which is to say you have to trust in muscle memory, as it were, to do the writing.

In the case of Matthias's laments we can see an accelerating stress on his craft from the anguishing trajectory of events, and an astonishing equipoise of response. In this respect, Matthias has been lucky in his masters, among whom I'd identify in particular the great British (Welsh) Modernist David Jones,[3] and John Berryman, Matthias's first writing teacher. The work of both these exceptional

---

2   Joseph Brodsky, ed., *The Essential Hardy* (Hopewell, NJ: Ecco Press, 1995), 44.
3   See Matthias's *Introducing David Jones* (Faber and Faber, 1980) and *David Jones: Man and Poet* (National Poetry Foundation, 1980).

craftsmen are studies in the possibilities of writing in the aftermath of trauma. T.S. Eliot, in his introduction (1961) to the paperback reissue of the Jones's masterpiece *In Parenthesis* (1937), notes that "The work of David Jones has some affinity with that of James Joyce . . . and with the later work of Ezra Pound, and with my own . . . . The lives of all of us were altered by [the First World] War." Looked at as the work of writers "altered," as Eliot puts it, by the First World War, Modernist writing can be cast as a registering of, a working through personal and historical PTSD: the language bends, strains, and cracks in the collision with the world-trauma.

Matthias had read John Berryman before he ever came across David Jones, and everything about Berryman and Berryman's work, especially the "Dream Songs" is important to Matthias. Michael Hofmann puts it perfectly: "Who knew English could encompass that flux" he says of the "Dream Songs"; "that whinny; those initially baffling, then canny and eventually unforgettable rearrangements of words; that irresistible flow of thoughts and nonthoughts of that degree of informed privateness?" Also: "I love the extremes of courtliness and creatureliness in the Dream Songs" which he observes "vary through every degree of lucidity and opacity"[4] All of which could be said of Matthias. In particular, I'd point to the easy mixing of registers, which appears everywhere in Matthias's writing, and the location of the writing, almost always, in the implicit setting of the long tradition of tales and

---

4   Michael Hofmann, Introduction, *The Dream Songs* by John Berryman (New York: Farrar, Straus and Giroux, 2014).

Romance (especially important in "Some of Her Things"), with their courtly rituals and diction.

In an explanatory endnote to "Complayntes for Doctor Neuro,"[5] of which the last section ("Good dream, good dream") is included here, Matthias confides that we should read the cycle as "a kind of dialogue with one of [his] favorite poets, Hilda Morley," one of the Black Mountain poets (Morley's husband, the Modernist composer Stefan Wolpe, suffered like Diana Matthias with Parkinson's). Morley and Matthias both write with the Greek and Roman classics often in mind, because in the Western tradition those tales say all there is to say about Fate, that is, about how to live with what, because we are human, befalls us. This struggle—to come to terms with what has happened—marks every word of Matthias's laments. How is he to do it? In the last poem of the "Complayntes" cycle he does it by reimagining Ovid's account of Baucis and Philemon. Although Ovid, as Matthias says, "can be as cruel in his metamorphoses / As some malign neurologist" his story of the old married couple Baucis and Philemon, poor peasants who are the only people in town to do right by the two disguised strangers Zeus and Hermes, is an unusually "gentle, generous story" (well, gentle and generous to Baucis and Philemon: Zeus kills everyone else in the town and burns it to the ground!). By the time we come to this last poem, Diana has been tormented in any number of ways by what has befallen her, the Parkinson's that steals her sleep, wrenches her limbs, scripts obscenities

---

5   The complete eleven-section poem can be found in *Complayntes for Doctor Neuro & Other Poems* (Shearsman Books, 2016).

in her speech, embeds her in illusory worlds of both pain and joy—though worse is yet to come—and so it is hard-earned by the poet and especially moving to the reader to come upon the poem's lovely close:

> And I was standing in a marble temple, and I
> Was not I. Beside me Serpent Aesculapius arose
> In flaming cloak. Diana spoke: *I am a linden tree*
> And what I was replied: *I have become an oak.*

"Living with a Visionary" is the poet's account of his, and Diana's, descent into hell. Her physical and mental afflictions worsen; what she once could recognize to be illusory apparitions and visions overtake her; she cannot be left alone. She does not sleep and does not eat. Covid strikes. Imprisoned at home Matthias and Diana sink into an exhaustion and confusion that must have beset, must be besetting many, many families. Both Diana and Matthias land in psychiatric wards; because of Covid they cannot see each other in person. Matthias only manages his release with the help of a "personal health-care advocate." Diana meanwhile is whisked off to a home near her daughter, which, although doubtless the right place for her, is far from South Bend. Matthias can only speak with her by phone. She contracts Covid, seems to recover, then relapses suddenly, and dies. Matthias never gets to see her.

It is paradoxical, one of the (many) ironic gifts of art that this harrowing story is narrated in Matthias's lucid, sinewy prose, his sturdily American and brilliantly managed English (he comes from a distinguished legal family in Ohio, the state whose language linguists once said embodied Standard American). But it's in "Some of Her Things," a fable in the form of a long prose poem, written shortly after Diana's death, that Matthias most powerfully, and poignantly, deploys his language and his craft. To borrow Michael Hofmann's word, it is a courtly threnody for lost time. It recalls Berryman's "Dream Songs" in its great effort to hold steady, to hold things together, to write subjects after verbs, just as it intermittently breaks down, and a manic or unmoored association kidnaps the writing. Matthias finds he is in the middle of the St. Joseph River, bound to save just seven things from a huge case containing all of Diana's clothes and favorite objects and memories and qualities of mind and person. Each of the poem's seven sections is devoted to one thing saved. At the outset Diana tells him to *"Do like Henry James"* who apparently had to dispose of Constance Woolson's things after her suicide.[6]

---

6   Woolson famously traveled everywhere with a huge array of objects, including:

> her tear vase
> her collection of ferns
> a picture of yellow Jasmine (her favorite flower)
> a weighing machine
> a stiletto from Mentone
> etchings of Bellosguardo and a red transparent screen used there
> a 1760 edition of the poems of Vittoria Colonna
> seven old prints bought by [her great-uncle James Fenimore] Cooper in Italy
> an engraving of Cooper
> a copper warming-pan from Otsego Hall given her by one of Cooper's daughters, Mrs. Phinney
> and a photograph of her cherished niece, Clare, which she hung in every room she occupied.

Lyndall Gordon, *Henry James: His Women and His Art* (Virago, 2012).

Woolson may have been in love with James? "Maybe James knew or maybe not. If it was the case, that is, and the world is everything that is the case." Because Matthias is in the river, and beside him is a giant case, his puns on "the case" (and his play with Wittgenstein) become a kind of meme in the work, an outlet, a permission to howl and bellow. "Punt's a long and narrow craft. Craft has several meanings, several anythings are maybe just in case. In case you wondered, in case you pay attention." In the seventh and last section of the poem, there's a moment of final clarity: "I suppose I stand midstream only in a dream, but I am broken to the point I can't tell . . . I've sent downstream all everything except the seven things I now will list. The case is closed.

The first thing I'll save is your magnolia tree
The next thing I'll save is your Schrödinger cat called Zeitgeist
I'll save for you your father's sailing boat
I'll save you all the wine in Jacob's well
I'll save your grandad's grandest prize: A By God Authentic Victoria Cross
I'll save your secret whispered in my ear
I'll save this bit of ice right in my heart."

This saving is the work of the lament, waging craft, imagination, song, devotion and heart's ache against loss, or maybe I should just say hope against hope. "Hilda Morley," Matthias writes, "called her Collected Poems *Cloudless at First,* and so it is for most of us. But the heavy weather will come."

45

ABOUT THE AUTHORS

JOHN MATTHIAS has published some thirty books of poetry, translation, criticism, and scholarship. For many years he taught at the University of Notre Dame, where he is still Editor at Large of *Notre Dame Review*. Shearsman Books publishes his three volumes of *Collected Poems*, as well as the uncollected long poem, *Trigons*, his two most recent volumes of shorter poems, *Complayntes for Doctor Neuro* and *Acoustic Shadows*, two books of memoirs and literary essays, and the novel *Different Kinds of Music*. Two collaborative books have been published by Dos Madres: *Revolutions* (with Jean Dibble and Robert Archambeau) and *Regrounding a Pilgrimage* (with John Peck). His most recent book is *Some Words on Those Wars* (Dos Madres, 2021).

IGOR WEBB was born in Slovakia and grew up in the Inwood neighborhood of New York City. His poems have appeared in the *New Yorker* and *Poetry* (Chicago). Among his publications are *Rereading the Nineteenth Century* (Palgrave Macmillan, 2010) and the memoir *Against Capitulation* (Quartet Books, 1984). His story "Reza Says," originally published in the *Hudson Review*, was selected as a Distinguished Story for *Best American Short Stories, 2012*. His most recent book, *Christopher Smart's Cat*, was published in 2018 by Dos Madres Press. Igor Webb is Professor of English at Adelphi University.